Vastu Shastra

VASTU SHASTRA

But what on earth is half so dear — so longed for —
as the hearth of home?

EMILY BRONTE

CAROLINE ROBERTSON

LANSDOWNE

Contents

Introduction

*Vastu is the result of thousands of years of research and development,
observing that one thing makes you ill and another does not.*
LAURIE BAKER, BRITISH ARCHITECT

Everyone thrives in a serene and secure living environment, yet very few know how to arrange their space so that it offers optimal health and happiness.

Ancient Indian sages developed a science of harmonious habitation, known as vastu shastra, which we can still apply today. Vastu, pronounced "vaastu," means "dwelling," and shastra, pronounced "shaastra," means "science." Vastu shastra is the ancient architectural art of design and building. It guides us in the creation of structures that will harness the most auspicious flow of energy into our lives. Promoting as it does a balanced symbiosis between humans, nature and buildings, vastu shastra is relevant to anyone who wants to enjoy a positive living environment.

Vastu shastra is a vast science, and, as vastu master V. Ganapathi Sthapati has remarked, "What is today spoken of by modern vastu pundits is only an infinitesimal part of the area covered by the shastra." Other topics covered in vastu shastra include the construction of temples, vehicles, furniture, sculpture, and works of art, as well as the planning of cities.

This book is an effort to simplify a complex science; it extracts the practical essence relevant to any layperson seeking to maximize his or her living space. This can apply to someone already living in an existing space, as well as someone who is designing an entire home. You will learn simple and effective tips for site selection, room orientation, landscaping, interior design, and rituals to attract positivity into your home.

Vastu shastra's main message is that, if we consciously mold our environment in consonance with universal energies, the environment will mold us in such a way that our true selves will effortlessly emerge. The good news is that you don't have to believe in vastu shastra for it to work. When you start to apply simple principles to your home, the results will speak for themselves.

An Ancient Science

The true basis for the more serious study of the art of architecture lies with those more humble indigenous buildings everywhere. Functions are truthfully conceived and rendered, invariably with a natural feeling. Results are often beautiful and always instinctive.
FRANK LLOYD WRIGHT, ARCHITECT

Architecture is always a spatial expression of a spiritual decision.
LUDWIG MIES VAN DER ROHE, ARCHITECT

ANCIENT ORIGINS

As with many of India's sciences, vastu shastra was traditionally taught by means of the oral tradition: it was transmitted from guru to disciple over thousands of years before being formally recorded. The myth states that originally, perhaps thousands of years ago, the god Brahma spoke the science to the celestial architect Vishvakarma. It was kept alive through a succession of erudite scholars and saints, including Lord Buddha. Textual references to vastu shastra can be found in the *Sthapatya-Veda*, a section of the Indian scripture the *Atharva-Veda*. There are also scores of treatises on vastu shastra, including the acclaimed *Manasara, Mayamata, Brihat Samhita, Vishvakarma Prakasha* and *Samarangana Sutradhara*.

Historical references to vastu shastra are present in the famous Indian epics the *Mahabharata* and the *Ramayana*. In the *Mahabharata*, the divine architect Maya built for the Pandavas a royal assembly hall that was instrumental in the defeat of an evil dynasty. The *Ramayana* describes Lord Rama choosing an exile cave according to vastu shastra principles, and taking guidance from Nala, Vishvakarma's son, when constructing the bridge from India to Sri Lanka.

The ancient Indian cities of Mohenjo-Daro and Pataliputra, dating back 3000 years, are shining examples of how vastu shastra was employed to create solid housing, boasting the world's first plumbing and temperature-controlled ventilation.

Most of India's enduring temples, including Tirupati, the richest temple in the world, were constructed according to the principles of vastu shastra. This science has also given us the magical musical pillars of Sri Meenakshi temple and the swinging minarets of Ahmedabad. Although of Muslim design, the Taj Mahal owes much of its success to the various vastu shastra aspects applied to its construction; it is one of the most frequently visited buildings in the world.

While you are reading this book, do bear in mind that it's virtually impossible to build a structure with perfect vastu. According to the ancient text the *Mayamata* (11:93), the potency of such a building is said to transmit a balancing vibration that reverberates throughout the world, creating perfection in the universe.

CULTURAL CONNECTIONS

Each blade of grass has its own spot on earth whence it draws its life, its strength,
and so is a man rooted to the land from which he draws his faith together with his life.
JOSEPH CONRAD IN LORD JIM

Research shows that vastu shastra principles were also embraced by the ancient Greeks, Romans, South Americans, Balinese, and Chinese, as exemplified by many of their temples. Similarly, many old places of worship in the Western world, such as St Paul's Cathedral, the Vatican, and Stonehenge, were constructed in accordance with vastu shastra's rules on dimension and orientation. The crucifixes and spires on the churches, coupled with the magnetic nature of their building materials, are said to act like antennae, tuning into positive vibrations from the biosphere. Their sacred ambience instills in visitors a sense of peace and spiritual upliftment.

Vastu Shastra and Feng Shui

If there is light in the soul there will be beauty in the person.
If there is beauty in the person there will be harmony in the house.
If there is harmony in the house there will be order in the nation.
If there is order in the nation there will be peace in the world.

CHINESE PROVERB

There are many similarities between vastu shastra and the Chinese system of feng shui:

Common belief	Vastu shastra variations	Feng shui variations
Space is not empty, but filled with luminous energy	Energy is known as 'prana'	Energy is known as 'chi'
The five elements are key factors in both systems	The elements are ether, air, fire, water and earth	The elements are wood, earth, water, fire and metal
The north–south orientation is exalted as the best layout for a building		
Awareness of the earth's natural electromagnetic emanations and the geopathic stresses that may result from poor placement over them		

There are also many differences between the two systems:

Focus: Feng shui places more emphasis on small cures such as mirrors and fish, whereas vastu shastra focuses on the big picture, involving the rearrangement of the floorplan and doors.

Mathematics: The systems use different mathematical dimensions; much of Vastu's mathematical scales are in accordance with the residents' measurements.

Placement: The placement of rooms, furniture and doors is often determined by numerology and astrology in feng shui, whereas vastu shastra only occasionally employs this approach.

Water: Vastu shastra advises that water should be in the north-east position, whereas feng shui says it should be in the front of the house regardless of direction (although water in the north is preferable).

Windows: Vastu shastra says it is best to have more windows and doors in the north, east and north-east, whereas feng shui warns against windows and doors in the north as this is considered a maleficent position. This belief is most likely influenced by the harsh winds that sweep yellow dust into the northern side of houses in China.

Ventilation: Vastu shastra has a concept of cross-ventilation whereby windows can be placed directly opposite each other. Feng shui warns against this practice, as it is said to promote dangerously rapid flowing chi, which will deplete residents' energy.

Space: In vastu shastra, the house is viewed as a "cosmic person" and this is the main determinant of room placement. Feng shui doesn't share the same spiritual concept of space.

Shape: Feng shui liberally uses the circular shape around the house, whereas vastu shastra rarely advises this use as it is considered unstable. The stable square or the rectangle with softened corners are preferred.

Vastu is about the physical, psychological
and spiritual order of the environment and its consonance
with the energies of the cosmic universe.
SASHIKALA ANANTH

Vastu Shastra in Action

The science underlying the technology of vastu is a science of manifestation.
It is a science of energy turning into material visual forms.
V. GANAPATHI STHAPATI

All of the ancient Indian sciences are founded on the understanding that the world consists of multifarious energy layers — from the superficial, material level to subtle spiritual sheaths. They emphasize that humans will be healthy and happy only when they attain a balanced co-existence between the subtle and gross forces in their external and internal worlds. Vastu shastra focuses strongly on the subtle energetic principles that are generally "unseen" by people, although evident through Kirlian photography and felt as the inherent "vibes" of a place.

Geomancers — people who study the earth energies of a site — are very accurate at distinguishing the subtle energetic forces impacting on a home, and work according to vastu shastra principles. In an effort to create the ideal structure, all of these energetic aspects are considered. The five main factors detailed in vastu shastra are solar science (the influence of the sun), the earth's magnetic field, wind force, gravitational pull, and cosmic planetary forces. These all have a role to play in formulating the ideal site and the ideal method of creating a new building or of maximizing an existing place. In Vastu, it is advised that a home captures the beneficial morning sun, as this means it is placed in alignment with the earth's magnetic field and is protected from malefic planetary and environmental influences. The solar science principles determining house placement were favored by many great thinkers, including Aristotle and Socrates. Vastu shastra is therefore based firmly in science rather than superstition.

A PERFECT BALANCE

A sthapati — a vastu shastra architect — combines a synergy of engineering, mathematics, art, astrology and astronomy to create a home that is in perfect balance with its surrounding environment. The land is assessed according to its geology and soil fertility and its relationship to other natural and man-made structures. The building is designed or adjusted with acute awareness of the earth's electromagnetic energy, the nine directions (north, south, east, west, center, south-east, north-east, south-west, and north-west) and the five universal elements (ether, air, fire, water and earth).

A structure is viewed as a living organism that, when properly constructed, forms a body around its own life force. It acts as a receptor for the harmonious interaction of these surrounding forces. A chaotic interaction of these energies would result in geopathic stress, which would affect the residents adversely. The balanced flow of these energies through a house can act to create a positive flow of energies in our bodies. This has been confirmed by experiments conducted by

Prabhat Poddar, an Indian architect and geobiologist. Just as a child is nourished and thrives in a healthy womb, so a resident is strengthened within the aura of a balanced home.

Vastu shastra involves more than just correct placement. It helps to increase our awareness of the subtle energy fields permeating everything. As writer Denise Linn explains, "Your home is not just a composite of materials thrown together for shelter and comfort. Every cubic centimeter, whether solid or seemingly empty space, is filled with infinite vibrating energy fields."

Benefits of Vastu Shastra

Sastrenaanena sarvasya lokasya paramamsukham
(Vastu brings ultimate happiness to the whole world.)
VISHWAKARMA Ó VASTUSHASTRA

Have you ever experienced a flood of difficulties after moving into a new home, or do you remember visiting a house that you couldn't wait to escape from? Chances are you were picking up on the negative energy of these environments, and this made you uncomfortable. Vastu warns of the dangers of living in a home that digresses from its major guidelines. Disease, relationship conflicts, poverty, infertility, accidents and obstacles to progress are just some things that can result from living in a discordant environment. Some people deal with this unconsciously, by spending all their time out, or by going on vacation as they know they will feel much better away from home; alternatively, some may notice they feel sick on weekdays in an unhealthy work environment, and healthier on the weekends.

The problem may have many origins, including poor placement, poor room orientation, an unsupportive surrounding landscape, harmful earth energies or negative energy from previous residents. The following chapters will help you to recognize and counteract possible detrimental influences so that you can align your home with principles that nourish positive growth and circumstances in your life.

Naturally our destiny and fortune are also influenced by factors other than our homes. None of the problems resulting from poor vastu are inevitable and insurmountable, nor are the benefits of good vastu shastra guaranteed. How we live in a home is just as important as the home we live in, which is why vastu shastra also gives guidelines for balanced living (see page 72). Adhering to the major precepts of vastu shastra is said to create happy house karma whereby all the residents enjoy optimal health, wealth and happiness.

Here are some of the specific benefits attributed to correct vastu shastra:

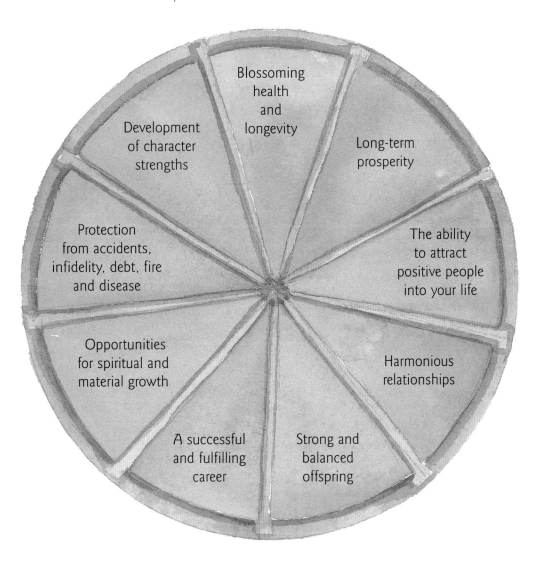

Blossoming health and longevity

Development of character strengths

Long-term prosperity

The ability to attract positive people into your life

Protection from accidents, infidelity, debt, fire and disease

Opportunities for spiritual and material growth

Harmonious relationships

A successful and fulfilling career

Strong and balanced offspring

Getting the Elements Right

*Vastu Purusha, or the subtle spirit which pervades the earth, is responsible
for the good and bad fortune of the building's residents.*
THE MAYAMATA

THE SPIRIT OF A SITE

The spirit embodying a site is known as the Vastu Purusha. Lying on a grid of
64 or 81 squares known as a mandala, this "cosmic landlord" is the geometric and
astrological basis for room designation and the positioning of walls. This rough
blueprint for architectural design is drawn in the form of a human likeness. The
human's head lies in the north-east in the mandala, the legs in the south-west,
the right hand in the north-west and the left hand in the south-east; other parts
of the body fill the square. Forty-five gods lie on top of him in their respective
areas. The Vastu Purusha symbolizes all the metaphysical and cosmological
premises of vastu shastra. The energy of the land must resonate with the ener-

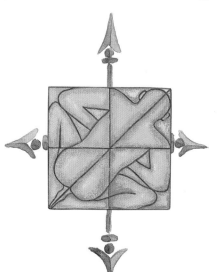

getic form of the mandala in order to
create a vibration that will enhance the
inhabitants' lives. As architect
Volwahsen has noted, "All existence is
reflected in this magic square."

The Hindu demigod of creation,
Brahma, proclaimed that whoever
constructs buildings on earth shall first
make offerings to Vastu Purusha in
order to invoke his blessings for a
dwelling that will bring all health and
harmony.

DIVINE DIRECTIONS

In vastu shastra, every aspect of a building should be allocated according to the specific earthly and cosmic influences governed by the directions. An example of this is that the kitchen is best in the south-east wing, which is where Agni, the god of fire, resides in the house. Guided by this model and armed with a compass, you can easily determine the proper place for each room and even the position for furniture in your building.

Each direction is associated with a specific god, planet and attribute.

Direction	God	Planet	Attribute and element
East	Indra, god of weather	Sun	Life, consciousness, intelligence, male children
West	Varuna, god of water	Saturn	Longevity, property, obstruction, resting, the unknown
North	Kubera, god of wealth	Mercury	Intellect, commerce, vocation, source of female offspring, prosperity, healing
South	Yama, god of death	Mars	Energy, logic, friends, enmity, meaning of life and death
North-east	Vishnu, supreme god	Jupiter	Teacher, husband, wealth, nourishing energies; WATER
South-east	Agni, god of fire	Venus	Beauty, wife/husband, comfort; FIRE
South-west	Durga/Niruti, goddess of destruction	Rahu	Disease, collective bad karma; EARTH
North-west	Vayu, god of wind	Moon	Personality, social life, emotions, intellect; AIR
Center	Brahma, god of creation	Ketu	Repose, contemplation and unity; ETHER

THE FIVE ELEMENTS

The dynamic dance of creation is choreographed by the all-pervading
rhythm of the five elements.
DR RAMA PRASAD, AYURVEDIC PHYSICIAN

From the beginning of recorded time, great thinkers such as Pythagoras and Hippocrates have expounded the five-element theory. According to this theory, the five elements of ether, air, fire, water and earth are present in every atom of the universe. Ether is the space that composes the majority of the universe. Every atom is 99.999% space. The quality of ether is present in the vibrations that create sound and gives things the appearance of solidity, even though they are predominantly space. As ether vibrates it fills with air, which provides movement and flow. Air creates friction, which creates the light and heat evident in fire. Fire liquefies matter and produces water. Evaporated water results in earth, the stabilizing force of the world.

More than just material elements, the five elements are the functional principles that govern everything in the macrocosm of the universe and the microcosm of our bodies. The harmonious flow of prana (energy) in our bodies is reliant on a healthy flow of elements in the atmosphere. Therefore it is vital to create a home that captures and circulates a healthy proportion of the five elements.

Element	Attribute	Shape	Function	Deficiency signs
ether	sound	dot	Subtle perception	Poor hearing and memory
air	touch	crescent	Movement	Breathlessness, tiredness, apathy
fire	sight	triangle	Transformation	Poor vision and appetite, coldness
water	taste	circle	Adhesion	Dryness, cracking joints, rigidity
earth	smell	square	Cohesion	Faint, ungrounded, deficiencies

Vastu shastra offers specific design and placement principles that support the balanced flow of elements. Here are some simple ways to ensure a healthy connection with these forces that weave our existence:

Element	Balancing exercises for elemental deficiency
ether	Play inspiring music (mantras, Mozart and Vivaldi are recommended), sing, avoid disturbing noises such as creaky doors, loud television, alarms
air	Burn uplifting scents, keep windows open, install a skylight in the middle of the building, avoid air conditioning, use a negative ionizer, practice yogic breathing (pranayama), keep indoor plants
fire	Watch the sunrise, gaze at a candle flame, let the morning sun into the house, install a fireplace, wear bright colors, exercise to sweat
water	Place a fountain in the north-east of the room or garden, keep indoor plants to balance humidity, make sure poor guttering, plumbing and rising damp are addressed, have an Epsom salts essential oils bath
earth	Walk in the garden/on the beach with bare feet, check the house foundations are stable, fix any gaps or cracks in walls and ceiling, do weight-bearing exercise, eat nourishing meals

Before rising saying the following prayer will increase your connection with the earth:

samudra-vasane devi parvata-stana-mandite
vishnu-patni namas tubhyam pada-sparsham ksamasva me
(Oh Mother Earth, consort of Lord Vishnu, Your garments are the seas and Your breasts are the mountains, salutations to You. Please excuse me for stepping on You.)

THE PERFECT PLOT

When we see our actions and our dwellings as hymns to the universe,
then we cannot help but build with joy and beauty
houses that are truly creations of love.
JOHN ARCHER IN THE HOME BUILDING EXPERIENCE

It is very important to have a clear vision of the style of house you want, and the environment you want to live in. You have to name it to claim it, so start by writing down the details of your dream home and environment. Look at other houses, browse through books and visit different architects before settling on the right style.

Whether you are starting a house from scratch or assessing a new home, there are some outstanding features of land that are auspicious in terms of vastu shastra. An ideal site will protect you from harsh weather patterns and channel in beneficial energies from the environment.

The focus in vastu shastra is on orientation. In general, the north and east are areas that receive energy, and the south-west is a zone that protects us from negative influences. There is a debate about whether these principles change for different hemispheres and weather patterns. Some vastu shastra and feng shui scholars recommend that the advice given on northern and southern directions be reversed in the southern hemisphere. However, the majority of vastu masters disagree with this, saying that the principles of house orientation and room placement are based on cosmological (all things pertaining to the cosmos) rather than terrestrial (aspects of earth) principles. In other words, the north/south alignment of the house and the room allocation are as fixed as the unchanging position of the Vastu Purusha. The sun rises in the east and sets in the west all around the world, so the east/west guidelines remain universal. However, if there are harsh winds coming from the south-west direction, the house needs to be sheltered by building high walls and planting sheltering trees.

Each home has its unique dynamics. Use your instincts and common sense to apply the elements of vastu shastra that enhance the home but, if they don't feel

right, play around until they do. Make sure the site is safe from electrical power-lines, bushfires, floods, landslides and chemical contamination from the air, soil, or water. It is always advisable to consult a vastu master before making the final purchase or plan.

The golden rule of Vastu is to keep the north, east and north-east lower in all levels and less loaded at any moment of construction as compared to other sides.
PROF. V.V. RAMAN, VASTU SCHOLAR

The major tenets of an auspicious site are as follows:

• Slope: Ideal land has a declining slope in the north and east and an elevation in the south and west.

• Land shape: The block of land should be rectangular or square, with angles at approximately 90°.

• Proportions: The land's ratio of width to length should not exceed 1:2.

• Borders: The house should sit with its borders parallel to those of the property borders.

• Projection: If there is a projection in the land, it should be in the north or the east.

• Mountains: Mountains on a property or bordering land, should be in the south, west, or south-west.

• Water: Bodies of water should be in the north, east, or north-east. However, fast-flowing water behind the house (either on the property or bordering land) is not recommended, as it will wash away prosperity. Land bordered by life-giving fresh water is considered healthier than land close to salt water, which dehydrates and heats the body. A house right on the beach is not recommended.

• Orientation: The house should face north, north-east, or east.

• Electromagnetics: The land's electromagnetic grid should be aligned with that of the house (a geomancer can determine this).

• Main road: This should be in the north, east, or north-east.

• Tall elements: Taller buildings, walls (on the property itself and surrounding properties), and trees should be in the south or west.

• Door: The main door to the house should be in the east or north.

• Light: The house should be more open and light in the north and east than in the south and west.

• High areas: If the house is higher in one area, this should ideally be the south or the west.

• Neighboring buildings: A house next to a cemetery, church, or police station is considered inauspicious. A house with buildings towering over it on the east or the north is not recommended.

The shape of a site is said to have an important impact on the property's auspiciousness.

Site shape	Result
Back of an elephant (Gajaprishta): elevated in the south, west, south-west and north-west	Prosperity and longevity
Back of a tortoise (Kurmaprishta): elevated in the center	Prosperity
Back of a demon: elevated in the north-east, east and south-east	Destruction

If any part of a plot is missing (cut out) or blocked (taken up by another property), vastu shastra warns that the following may result:

Plot cut in this direction	Will result in
South-east	Financial problems and unhappy relationships
North-west	Loss of money, food, or possessions
North-east	Immoral acts committed, a bad reputation gained
South-west	Danger to sons and thwarted success

SECURITY IN THE SOIL

A fertile, clayey, fragrant and even land with medicinal plants, trees and climbers
is the harbinger of wealth, happiness and peace.
BRIHADVASTUMALA (1.77–8)

A site with rich, fertile soil is a conducive environment for setting down stable roots, planting the seeds of future dreams and reaping the rewards of your efforts.

Traditionally, vastu experts assessed the soil by examining its color, taste, smell and texture. In modern times we can employ the services of a soil survey to analyse the soil for pH, fertility, nitrogen, clay content, chemicals, heavy metals, minerals and porosity.

Land that has sweet-smelling soil and an even texture is considered most lucky. Land with white ants, beehives, rats, bones, sand, hard stones, cracks, ditches and dryness should be rejected. Modern geomancers have found that beehives, anthills and hard stones, such as granite, tend to be found where there are harmful junctions in the earth's electromagnetic lay lines, supporting the vastu shastra theories. A home built on an area that formerly held water is also considered inappropriate.

You can conduct some simple vastu shastra tests to ascertain the quality of the soil:

1 Dig a hole with measurements 3 ft (1 m) long x 3 ft (1 m) wide x 3 ft (1 m) deep.

2 Fill the trench with water. When the water becomes still, float a flower in the middle. If the flower rotates in a clockwise direction, this indicates that positive energy pervades the land. In the northern hemisphere, if the flower rotates counter-clockwise, this isn't considered a good omen. In the southern hemisphere, however, counter-clockwise rotation of the flower is a good sign.

3 If the pit still retains some water after at least 12 hours and hasn't developed any cracks in this period, this indicates that the soil is of very high quality.

4 Fill up the pit with the previously excavated earth. If there is excess soil remaining, this is a sign that the land will bring prosperity. If there is insufficient soil to fill the pit, this suggests that the land will not support abundance of wealth and prosperity. If there is just enough soil to fill the hole, the occupants will enjoy a healthy, balanced life.

It is also a good idea to sow some seeds in order to find out how quickly they will germinate in this soil. The faster they germinate, the more fertile the soil is. The greenery on neighboring properties will also give you a fair idea of the region's soil quality. If the soil is irredeemable, remove the top 6-ft (2-m) layer and refill with fresh, fertile soil.

BEAUTIFUL BUILDING MATERIALS

It is most wonderful to know that when a building has outlived its life
it can return to the earth. When you work with mud and hard plaster the walls,
it is like forming an external skin,
it is every bit of the building that embodies the human spirit,
the cyclic care of the building being a part of the act of living.
REVATI KEMATH

Since vastu shastra considers the house to be a living organism unto itself, much like a person's third skin (the first being body and second clothes), it should be constructed from natural, "breathing" materials such as wood or earth. This will ensure the preservation of the life of the building and its inhabitants. Some natural building materials, such as sandstone and earth, emanate healing, positive energies which can conduct a healing vibration throughout the house. Conversely, there are building materials which attract negative concentrations of energy such as steel reinforced pillars, granite, quartz and concrete.

Go through this checklist before purchasing building materials; also see "Healing the Home" page 68. Are they:

• free from chemical pollutants, radioactive energy and harmful electromagnetic energy?

• resistant to bacteria, viruses, molds, termites and other harmful micro-organisms or allergens?

- able to provide protection from excessive light, heat, cold, wind, water and sound?

- able to prevent static electricity from being conducted?

- available in abundance, and renewable?

- durable, long lasting and easy to maintain and repair?

The most commonly used materials in vastu shastra are earth and wood, since they fit the above criteria when carefully selected and prepared. Wood is a direct gift from nature and brings the breath of life to a house. It can endure for thousands of years, and often grows more attractive with age. Timber absorbs carbon dioxide and doesn't require the use of chemicals in its production.

With the global deforestation crisis, it is always best to use locally grown plantation timbers, or at least to be sure that the timber is from new-growth forest rather than from old-growth forests or rainforests. Because wood absorbs any negative vibrations from the surroundings, vastu shastra doesn't recommend the use of recycled timber unless you are sure that the previous users had a pure energy. A ritual for cutting down the tree for building, involves a short prayer asking the tree's spirits to leave, and requesting permission to cut it down. Once the tree is felled it is only considered auspicious if it falls to the east or the north.

Ancient vastu shastra books hail the superiority of certain trees, including *Areca catechu, Shorea robusta, Dalbergia sissoo* and *Madhuca longifolia*. Oak has been used in vastu buildings because of its strength, durability,

impermeability, resistance to molds and insects, and ability to stain to beautiful rich hues.

The following are some hardy building plantation timbers that fulfill the vastu shastra principles: Cypress pine (*Callitris* spp.), radiata pine (*Pinus radiata*), hoop pine (*Aracaria cunningbamii*), poplar (*Populus* spp.), Blackbutt (*Eucalyptus pilularis* spp.), Sydney blue gum (*Eucalyptus salinga* sm.), spotted gum (*Eucalyptus citriodora, e. maculata*), Mana gum (*Eucalyptus uiminalis*), rose gum (*Eucalyptus grandis*), jarrah (*Eucalyptus marginata*), red ironbark (*Eucalyptus sideroxylon*) and silvertop stringybark (*Eucalyptus leavopinia*). Be aware that most commercial woods are chemically treated. An alternative is to use a borax wood impregnation treatment, resin oil, or a beech wood distillate to protect the wood against molds and termites.

Mud bricks, which have undergone a recent revival, are a viable option. The buildings of some of the longest surviving colonies of Mesopotamia, Egypt, Greece and Italy were constructed from mud bricks. Once properly fired, these are simple to construct, readily available, durable, renewable, effective insulators, low cost, and rot and termite proof. They have a wonderful organic look to them, as if they have grown from the earth itself. Vastu texts advise that the soil used for making mud bricks should be swollen and mixed with a bit of red sand. Such soil should ideally be free of gravel, roots and bones, and have a homogenous color. After being mixed with herbs it is baked. Bricks that aren't damp some time after being immersed in water are considered worthy of use.

Stone is suitable for warm climates, and should be dense, smooth and its length greater than its depth.

LAYING THE FOUNDATIONS

Traditionally, a jyotish, or Vedic astrologer, will outline certain auspicious times for laying the foundation stone and for commencing and completing construction. Vastu shastra experts claim that, if commencement of building is supported by a positive alignment of the planets, the house will be assured of a stable, durable and fortunate future. If important construction phases are undergone during a maleficent planetary alignment, however, there may be difficulties with construction and other problems in the future.

Once the auspicious times have been outlined certain ceremonies are then performed, preferably by a Hindu priest, to invoke the blessings of divine forces and to appease the home's environmental energies.

The ceremony for laying the foundation stone should be in the north-east. The stone should then be taken to the south-west, where the construction should actually begin. A Hindu priest would traditionally perform ceremonies called Vastu Shanti and Navagraha Homam, where certain precious stones, metals and grains are placed on the land to ensure the grace of celestial forces.

Once the construction work is complete, a traditional house-warming celebration, known as Griha Pravesha, should be held. Here the blessings of the gods are once again invoked, and all those involved in the construction of the house will be given presents and a feast in gratitude.

Close to Home

ROADS LEADING TO THE PROPERTY

The roads that terminate at the home are called "veedhi shoolas" which literally translates as road arrows. The direction they are coming from determines whether they harbor negative or positive energy.

• A road pointing straight at the property, such as at a T-intersection with the road directed at the middle of the home, is said to create danger to residents.

• Roads pointing at the home from the following direc-
tions are acceptable: north side of north-east, south-east on the south side, north-west on the west wall.

• Roads pointing at the home from the east side of the south-east, north side of the north-west and south side of the south-west are unfavorable.

• A house at the end of a dead-end street is considered unlucky as it will lead to stagnation and unfulfilled potential.

• A site with roads parallel to all sides is considered good vastu shastra, although if the roads are busy this will pose a danger to children and increase noise and air pollution levels.

- Four roads pointing directly to the home is considered bad vastu shastra.

- Roads in the east, west or north or north-east parallel to the house are also considered auspicious.

- If the only road pointing to the site is in the south or south-west direction, it is connected with poverty.

Knowing your Neighbors

Love thy neighbors as thyself but choose your neighbors.
Louise Beal

What may appear to be a little piece of paradise can turn into a living hell if your neighbors are difficult. Before you make the huge investment of purchasing a property, it is especially important to check that your neighbors will be tolerable. This may sound difficult, but will be nowhere near as difficult as living next door to nightmare neighbors. You could even make a friendly visit to meet your prospective neighbors, inquiring about the neighborhood. Observing their house and behavior will perhaps give you some indication of their nature.

Positive thoughts, words and deeds towards your neighbors can help establish smooth relations. As Mother Teresa advises, "Be the living expression of God's kindness: kindness in your face, kindness in your eyes, kindness in your smile."

Inside the House

The house is more than a box in which we live;
it is a soul activity to be retrieved from the numbness of the world of modern objects.
Each place of the house, each room, hallway, closet, stair and alcove
is a distinct structure that animates different aspects of the soul.
CLARE COOPER IN HOUSE AS A MIRROR OF THE SELF

THE ROOM PLAN

The home is a place that accommodates our natural activities and tendencies. It should have an atmosphere that brings out the best in us, mentally, physically and spiritually.

Well-designed rooms will inspire you to perform the activities for which they were intended. Imagine entering your bedroom and feeling a mood of relaxation and tenderness. Or imagine a kitchen that excites your cooking creativity, a living room that helps you to socialize and unwind, a dining room that stimulates your appetite and a study that inspires your intellectual drive.

According to vastu shastra, rooms should be designated according to their direction and the activities conducive to that region. An ideal floor plan has the following elements:

• A home that is either square or rectangular, although it may have an extension in the north or east area.
• A front entrance in the north or east, preferably not facing the bathroom with a toilet.
• An open, light foyer or courtyard near the middle of the home.
• A living room slightly larger than other rooms in the north.
• A dining room in the mid-west region.
• Bedrooms in the south-west, west and north-west.
• A kitchen in the south-east zone
• A study in the west or south-west.
• A bathroom with a toilet in the north-west or east.
• A meditation room in the north-east corner.

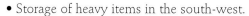

- Storage of heavy items in the south-west.
- Storage of valuables and medicines in the north.
- Area for keeping pets in the north-west.
- Attic or vertical extension in the south or west.
- Basement or swimming pool in the north or east.
- Stairs in the south-west area of a room or of the home.
- More windows and doors in the north and east than in the south and west.
- A sloping roof, rather than a flat roof, for better drainage and energy flow.

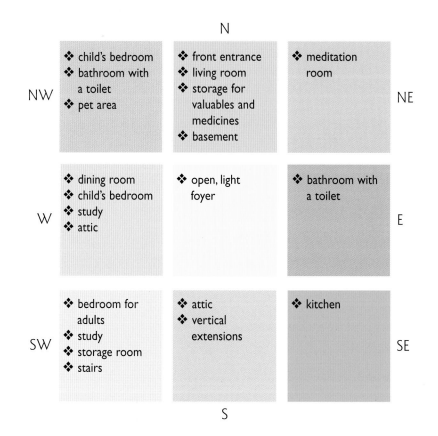

N

NW
- ❖ child's bedroom
- ❖ bathroom with a toilet
- ❖ pet area

- ❖ front entrance
- ❖ living room
- ❖ storage for valuables and medicines
- ❖ basement

- ❖ meditation room

NE

W
- ❖ dining room
- ❖ child's bedroom
- ❖ study
- ❖ attic

- ❖ open, light foyer

- ❖ bathroom with a toilet

E

SW
- ❖ bedroom for adults
- ❖ study
- ❖ storage room
- ❖ stairs

- ❖ attic
- ❖ vertical extensions

- ❖ kitchen

SE

S

THE GRAND ENTRANCE

Facing you, O House, you are facing me, I approach you peacefully:
Sacred Fire and Water are within, the main doors to Cosmic Order.
ATHARVA-VEDA (1.x3)

Approaching a house is like meeting a person. Someone with a warm, open, friendly expression will instantly put you at ease; similarly, a house with a welcoming entrance will create a positive first impression and attract good fortune into the home.

The ideal location for the front door is the north, east, or north-east. Keep the passage to the door free of clutter, bright and smooth. A door with a small porch will pull more prana (energy) into your home. Cleanse this area (front path and front door) with sandalwood, kum kum and turmeric paste every morning. Alternatively, wash it down with a mix of water and essential oil — frankincense, sage, sandalwood, or lavender.

A tradition still followed in India is the application of an intricate pattern known as a "kolam" or "rangoli." Every morning this pattern is applied to replace symbolically the night's ignorance with the day's enlightenment. An auspicious design may involve flowers, shells, gods, yantras or Sanskrit phrases. The pattern is applied to the ground in front of the door using flour such as rice, red lentil or colored chalk. This design is a metaphor for universal order, and attracts beneficial energies from the surrounding environment.

The door itself should be from a single type of wood, preferably not recycled. If it is in two pieces, they should be of equal size. The minimum dimensions for the door are 6 ft (2 m) high and 2 ½ ft (0.75 m) wide. However, many old vastu houses have a raised threshold and a low door so you are forced to bow in reverence to the home's sanctity on entering. It is considered bad vastu shastra to have a door below ground level. If this is unavoidable, place a light pointing upward at the doorway to reduce depressing influences.

Carvings or paintings on the door should not depict fierce animals, war scenes, nudes or any distressing subjects. A door made of glass or louver boards

is too fragile, as it won't give the house sufficient security. Install a wire security door to counteract this.

The front door that opens clockwise into the house channels more energy inside. It is considered bad luck to have certain things directly in line with the front door, such as a cemetery, sharp angles from buildings or vehicles, a pole, a bathroom with a toilet, stairs, a funeral home, a T-intersection, a traffic circle (roundabout), garbage, knives, or a sink. A noisy door or one that opens and closes on its own is not desirable — this suggests the residents are not in control of their environment. If opening the lock requires a lot of fiddling and jiggling with the key, this may result in irritating obstacles in the residents' lives.

The positive potency of the front door may be enhanced by auspicious motifs such as pictures or statues of Laksmi, the goddess of fortune, Ganesha, the elephant god who removes obstacles, or Krishna, the god of devotion. Place these above the outside of the front door. Strings of mango leaves and marigolds can adorn this area on special occasions. Have nothing on the inside of the door, as anything attached here will symbolically prevent positive external influences from entering. You could brighten up the front door with fresh paint, a pair of auspicious plants of a species, such as holy basil, or a mirrored fabric door piece.

The front door should preferably open to a large bright foyer, or into the living room. This is the area where many people will take off their shoes; this keeps out impurities from the external environment while enabling us to absorb the grounding earth energies of the house. As C. G. Jung said, "When you walk with naked feet, how can you forget the earth?" Keep shoes in a closed wall closet (cupboard) or in the nearest room, rather than blocking the front entrance.

THE FOYER

Having a light and open area at the entrance to the house will make the transition from outside to inside smoother. According to vastu shastra, a foyer or inner courtyard is the best entrance point into a home. The concept of the inner courtyard or atrium is common to the ancient architecture of Greece, Italy and Asia. The very word for this in Persian is "pairidaeza," or "paradise." The inner courtyard is mythically the location of the building's soul, hence it is considered a sacred area, where spiritual rituals and family gatherings should take place.

The middle of the courtyard can have a fountain or pool for catching rain water, but large trees should not be grown here. In modern times, a skylight in the center of the building is the next best thing to an atrium.

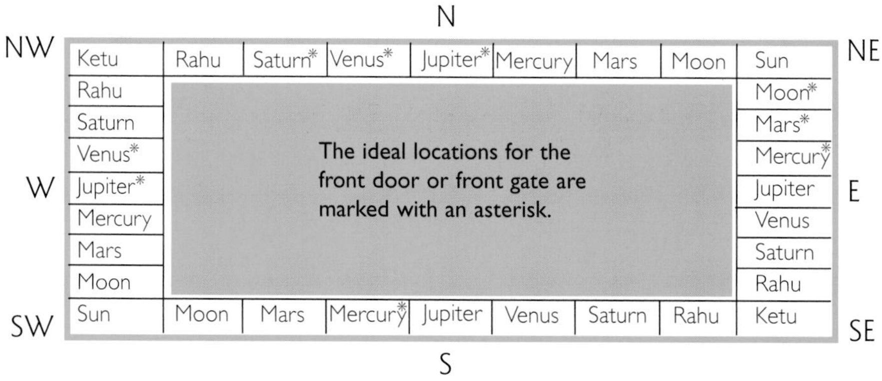

			N					
Ketu	Rahu	Saturn*	Venus*	Jupiter*	Mercury	Mars	Moon	Sun
Rahu								Moon*
Saturn								Mars*
Venus*			The ideal locations for the					Mercury*
Jupiter*			front door or front gate are					Jupiter
Mercury			marked with an asterisk.					Venus
Mars								Saturn
Moon								Rahu
Sun	Moon	Mars	Mercury*	Jupiter	Venus	Saturn	Rahu	Ketu

NW (top left) — NE (top right) — W (middle left) — E (middle right) — SW (bottom left) — S (bottom center) — SE (bottom right)

THE LIVING ROOM

There is brightness all around when there is love at home.
There is joy in every sound when there is love at home.
Time will softly, sweetly glide when there is love at home.
K. Sri Dhammananda in Why Worry

An ambience of comfort and unity in the living room will enhance relationships between household members. Ideally sited in the northern wing, the living room is the recreational and social heart of the home.

Keep electronic equipment in the south-east corner. If the television set is in a cabinet with a door, less time will be wasted watching it, and it won't distract people on social visits. Television in the north-east could lead to eye trouble, and in the north-west can become addictive. When not watching television, turn it off at the electrical outlet; while on, it will continue beaming electromagnetic waves to the remote control, cutting the room's energy fields.

Have furniture and heavy plants in the south-west, and mirrors on the north or east walls. The furniture should be against a wall and have gently rounded edges, though furniture should not be circular. Large "floating" furniture is said to contribute to the presence of volatile and unstable relationships. Too much furniture will stagnate the room's energy and create an uncomfortable, claustrophobic feeling. Ideally there should be more windows on the east and north side than on the west or south side. A fan in this room can also assist with good ventilation. Keep children's toys in the north-west, and hanging furniture in the north or east. Group photos of residents and auspicious pictures (see "Artwork" on page 57) can be placed in the north-east of this room to promote a sense of household harmony and co-operation.

37

THE STUDY

Placement of the room, desk and chair for study can enhance concentration and memory. Having the study on the west side of the south-west side of the home with the chair facing east, north, or north-east will give you the best planetary influences for brain power. The presence of Mercury increases intelligence, the moon cultivates fresh insights, Jupiter fires ambition and Venus encourages talent. The computer desk can be in the south-east, so long as your back isn't to the door.

A pyramid-shaped roof heightens mental focus and stamina, but isn't suitable in a room where you sleep or relax. A bookshelf and plant are best in the south-west or west. The north-east corner is the ideal place for a small fountain or a negative ionizer to counterbalance the harmful electromagnetic energy emitted by electrical appliances. This is also a good area for a picture of Saraswati, the goddess of learning, Ganesha, the god who removes obstacles to desired goals, or someone who is a source of inspiration.

Fluorescent lights directly overhead drain our energy. If the chair overlooks a view or the room has too many decorative items, your attention could be distracted. Overhead bookshelves and hooks pointing at the desk are said to inhibit mental clarity. The room should be bright and well-ventilated.

The Inner Sanctum

*Within you there is a stillness and sanctuary to which
you can retreat at any time and be yourself.*
HERMANN HESSE IN SIDDHARTHA

The inner sanctum is a sacred space where you can reconnect with the yearnings of your spirit. This is a quiet and nurturing area, or a room where you can take time away from external demands and negative influences in order to regain inner clarity, strength and focus.

The most conducive area for this is the north-east wing of the house, or a corner of a room such as the living room. If you feel drawn to a particular spiritual mentor or form of divinity, representations can be placed in the east of the room facing west, so that you can face east while praying or meditating. Place candles, crystals, incense and flowers before them to invoke their blessings.

A window in the north and east of this room will attract the beneficent influences of the divine. This area can be minimally furnished, since it is the "head" area of the house and should not be suffocated by objects. Heavy furniture such as closets (cupboards) can be placed in the south-west of this region.

Medicine was traditionally kept in the northern room of the home next to the prayer room. A pyramid-shaped roof in the inner sanctum heightens awareness and concentration, facilitating an easier connection with higher forces.

A small sound system can go in the south-east. Cushions, meditation stools, or exercise mats can be placed so that the practitioner faces east.

FINE DINING

Vastu shastra places the dining room in the mid-west room. The west is governed by Saturn, a planet that cultivates positive eating habits. A round table is not advised, as this is said to incite debates and arguments. Traditionally, meals were taken from small individual tables, which were stacked after each meal to leave more space in the dining room.

Sitting on the floor in the yogic thunderbolt position (vajrasana) is also considered the most conducive position for good digestion. Another tradition is to eat with the hands off plates made from banana or lotus leaves. This will give the food a special flavor, and save on washing up!

Paintings of lush flora and food will help to stimulate the appetite in this room. It is preferable to sit facing east while eating, and to observe these guidelines given in order to get the most from your meals.

• It is best to eat only when you are really hungry, and when the previous meal has been fully digested (roughly 3–4 hours).

• It is recommended that you empty the bowels and bladder before eating. It is a sign of ill health to empty the bowels immediately after eating.

• Simple hygiene is important to avoid illness. Wash hands, face and feet. Avoid taking a full shower or having a swim within three hours after eating, as this will draw the circulation away from the digestion.

• Pleasant company, conversation and surroundings are conducive to a contented mind. This will assist digestion.

• Express your gratitude in the form of a prayer, directed either to a higher power, or to the people who helped provide the meal.

• Eating is more than a vitamin-mineral intake program involving only the food and the mouth. We should involve our minds and sense organs in the act of eating. Eating is healing. We are worshiping the fire within through eating. Inhale the aromas, listen to the music of chewing, feel the food's texture, enjoy its colors and experience its taste in a meditative way. Take time to appreciate the sound, the aroma, the texture, the appearance and the taste of the food. This will make eating complete and digestion perfect.

• Eat at a moderate speed, taking care to chew each mouthful at least 10–20 times.

• Small quantities of warm drinks or drinks at room temperature will encourage efficient absorption, elimination and the action of the digestive fire.

• Remember that the stomach is only the size of a fist. To avoid over-eating, fill your stomach half-full with solids and a quarter-full with liquids, and leave the remaining quarter empty for space to circulate to aid digestion. Two handfuls of food are suggested as the ideal quantity at each meal.

• Ayurveda, the Indian medical science, recommends that we avoid heavy labor, exercise or mental work for at least thirty minutes after eating. A slow walk for five minutes is advised.

• Sleep should be strictly avoided for two hours after eating as this causes the formation of toxins. However, you may lie on the left side for up to fifteen minutes. The yoga posture vajrasana (thunderbolt) is also a good sitting position for aiding digestion after eating.

The Bedroom

The bedroom is a snug nest, a place where we can let down our guard and shut out the external world. Here we can regenerate and reconnect with our partners.

Ideally, the bedroom is just that: a room with a bed and little else. It should be free from any distractions and disturbances; it should promote the deep sleep essential for mental and physical stability. The quietest and darkest room in the house is most conducive to this.

Vastu shastra advises that the best bedroom location is in the south-west for the head of the household, the west for children and the north-west for guests. Bedrooms on the ground floor are said to promote a deeper sleep. The heads of the household should always have the upstairs bedroom if there is one, as this is a position of power. In general, bedrooms in the south-east are related to anger and mood swings, whereas those in the north-east induce emotional hyper-sensitivity and disease.

The bed itself should be placed on the south or west side, not touching the walls. The head can point to the south, west or east, but never to the north. When we sleep with our heads to the north, the north pole disturbs the circu-lation, as the iron in our body is drawn to the head. This contributes to hyper-activity, bad dreams and poor sleep in general. Your sleep will be more restful if the door is visible from the bed. Having your feet facing south is also a bad omen as south is the direction of death. This is why many cultures position their dead people in this manner. Having your feet facing the door is also symbolic of death, as a corpse is always carried out feet first.

Ensure that your feet are not pointing to a sacred picture or object, as this is seen as offensive. Ideally, the woman should sleep on the left side as this repre-sents the ida (feminine channel); the man should sleep on the right, the pingala, masculine side. The healthiest mattress will have a chiropractic or physiothera-pist's seal of excellence, and the pillow should be made of natural fibres so it sup-ports the curve of the neck. Be careful not to place your bed over the earth's lay lines, under an object pointing downward like a sharp lightshade or an exposed beam, or over an underground pipe or stream.

It is advisable to turn off any electrical appliances in the room before sleep. They emit energetic forces which can disturb your natural flow of prana (life force). Less is definitely more in the bedroom. The stimulating energy of television, a computer, or work-related things is contrary to the sedating ambience desirable here. If you have to keep these objects in this room, cover them with a screen or store them in a cupboard.

Keep bookshelves or a reading desk in the south-west, electrical things in the south-east and small framed pictures in the north-east. Keep mirrors out of view of the bed as they tend to focus energy toward you, disturbing sleep. Having a skylight overhead, or sleeping next to a large window, can have the same effect because of lunar energy — although this is good for women who want to keep their menses regular. Attached bathrooms are not recommended but, if essential, it should be in the south or west of the room.

Lighting can be pinkish and decentralized. Room colors are ideally in muted hues, unless you want to evoke passion, in which case you could use deeper shades of purples and reds.

THE KITCHEN

*The kitchen is the base of all domestic operations, and the one place
where we can "act locally" and play an active part in protecting the health
of ourselves and that of the wider environment.*
DAVID PEARSON IN THE NATURAL HOUSE BOOK.

The kitchen is the stomach of the home. A kitchen that facilitates easy, nutritious
meal preparation ensures the health and happiness of the household. The principles of digestion and cooking are governed by the element of fire, hence the
kitchen should be placed in the south-east where fire dominates. The plan for the
kitchen applies irrespective of room location. The worst place for the kitchen is
the north-east; this is said to cause all aspects of life to go up in flames.

When you are designing your kitchen, your primary concerns should be to
maintain a high standard of cleanliness, provide a large area for food preparation,
and ensure the safety of the cook. The focused consciousness of the cook is a
vital ingredient in cooking. To help, keep the kitchen very clean and organized
and prevent people from drifting in and out. Bright flowers, windowsill herbs
and uplifting music will also help to make this room a pleasant place.

The electric range of cookware or kitchen appliances are traditionally placed
on the south-east side, not touching the walls. It isn't advisable to place them
opposite the entrance door or under an exposed beam. If the cook faces east
when cooking, the food is said to be imbued with a heavenly flavor. The best
medium for cooking is cow dung, which is naturally antiseptic. The next best is
wood, then gas; electricity ranks last. The sink and refrigerator should preferably
not be adjacent or opposite to the stove as this will create a clash between the
fire and water elements. A counter between them, or a gap, will help to reduce
this problem.

If you want to maintain hygiene and preserve a calm atmosphere for the cook,
eating in the kitchen is not recommended. If you do need to have a dining table,
place it in the middle of the kitchen or in the south-west corner.

44

More and larger windows in the east will help to increase the fire element as the sun's rays stream in. A window or door in the west will facilitate cross-ventilation.

The refrigerator is ideally positioned in the north-west or south-west, and the sink and taps in the north-east. A storage cupboard is suited to the south and west sides. Cooking utensils hanging from the roof pose a symbolic threat to the cook, and vastu shastra directs them to be kept in drawers in the south-west or south-east.

One way cooks can increase their attentiveness and devotion to cooking is by preparing the meal without tasting it and then sanctifying the completed meal by offering it to the higher source before serving it to everyone. This will transform cooking and eating into a sacred experience, whereby the prasadam (spiritualized food) offers nourishment for the body and soul. This is a common practice in many Hindu households and is similar to the practice of saying grace. A small plate and eating utensils are placed in the east or north of the kitchen together with a picture or statue of the chosen divinity. Before anyone takes the meal, a portion is served and ritually offered with gratitude on the altar. Leave this for a few minutes and then clear away, wash the crockery and mix the sanctified meal back into the main pots. Now everyone can partake. This practice is also said to nullify bad karma incurred by the killing of plants for food.

THE BATHROOM

One of the nicest features of the vastu-inspired architecture of Bali is the outdoor bathroom. This concept was developed with a view to keeping impurities outside the house, just as we prefer to store our toxic garbage outside our houses. In India in the past, people would cleanse themselves after a day's work in a nearby river or the outdoor bathroom before entering the house. The toilet for internal cleansing was always a separate area from the area for external cleansing or bathing.

If your bathroom with a toilet is indoors, a good compromise to reduce bad luck from entering the house is to keep the room small, the seat down and the door closed. Place this room in the north-west or east of a house. It is considered taboo to place this room in the north-east, and poverty inducing to have it opposite the front door. It is also considered bad vastu to have it opposite the meditation room, the kitchen, or the dining room. The traditional vastu shastra squatting toilet and bidet have been shown to enhance complete evacuation and decrease the incidence of haemorrhoids, polyps and constipation.

The shower and bathtub can be in the north-east, the sink and closet (cupboard) in the west, and a heater and other electrical appliances in the southeast. A chlorine filter over the shower head and bathtub taps will reduce the toxic effects of excess chlorination. Terracotta non-slip tiles are practical on the floor, as they reduce mold and bacteria and absorb humidity. If there is a drainage slope in the floor tiles, this should decline toward the north-east. Ferns or other indoor plants will help to reduce humidity and freshen the air.

A big bath can provide the best relaxation therapy money can buy. Regular Epsom salts and essential oil baths will help to remove the effects of electromagnetic exposure and stress, lulling you into a deep sleep.

STORING VALUABLES

The storage area for valuables or money is best placed in the south-west corner of the northern room of the home. The door of the safe can open to the north or north-east to attract the prosperous influence of Kubera, the Lord of wealth. According to vastu shastra, keeping the safe opposite a door or under a window is not secure. The best safe sits with stability on a foundation, rather than having legs. The safe should be kept away from cobwebs and should not be under an overhead exposed beam. Nothing heavy should bear down on the top of it. This would obstruct the divine forces of prosperity from flowing in. Keeping a yantra or sacred symbol of Kubera, the god of wealth, or Laksmi, the goddess of fortune, in the safe is said to preserve and multiply prosperity.

THE STAIRS

The quality of the stairs in the home reflects the stability and support in its residents' lives. Long, narrow, spiraling stairs with gaps in between are not good vastu shastra as they represent fragility, loss of vitality and dwindling prosperity. The ideal stairs are wide, gently curving and located in the south-west area of the home or room. Odd numbers are the most auspicious number for stairs, preferably those that when divided by three have a remainder of two — for example, 11, 17, or 23. If the stairs spiral, they should revolve clockwise. Stairs located at the center of the house, in the north-east, opposite the entrance, or above a bedroom are considered bad luck. Steps should ideally proceed from east to west or from north to south. Elevators, or lifts, are also best located on the south-west side.

THE WINDOWS

Windows are to a house what the orifices are to our body. They are essential for receiving a harmonious flow of elements into the house, and supporting the life and longevity of the structure and its residents. To take advantage of the morning sun, add more windows in the east of the house. There should also be windows in the north-west and the north.

The windows in a home should preferably all be made of the same wood, with square or rectangular frames at 90° angles. Arched windows are considered incomplete forms, and are therefore not recommended. The same applies to windows with lines or motifs that point downward. Windows opening outward harness more prana than windows that open upward or inward. The ratio of windows to doors should be no more than three to one.

Small window boxes with plants can be placed on windowsills, but they should not block light from entering the house. Noisy blinds or curtains flapping in the wind will disturb the serenity of a home and are said to attract maleficent spirits.

THE BALCONIES

Balconies should be of equal width, and run all around the house. If this is not possible, they should be on the north and the east.

THE GARAGE

Motor vehicles are very convenient when they run smoothly, but are an endless source of headaches when they play up. In order to channel the best energy support for your vehicle, vastu shastra advises that it should be parked in the south-east or north-west of the house, preferably in a garage with walls separate from those of the house. Placing the vehicle so it faces east or north is also recommended. A toilet or sink in the garage is not good vastu shastra, as the water element will counteract the fire needed to support engine (motor) function. The garage should ideally not touch the boundary walls of the house, and should be no more than half of the length of the house.

The Finishing Touches

No matter how perfect a room is architecturally,
and no matter how well the furniture has been planned,
the space doesn't come to life until it is filled with beautiful objects, flowers and art.
NOEL JEFFREY, INTERIOR DECORATOR

DECOR

It is only when we add our unique decorating panache to a house that it really becomes a home. The style in which we decorate a space reflects our personalities, individual preferences and creative passions. It is an indication of our inner life and the way we perceive ourselves.

Decorating according to a lifestyle magazine or entrusting the decor of your home entirely to an interior decorator will contradict your own instinctive sense of harmony and aesthetics. Trust your preferences for color, textures and shapes — they are born from an intuitive drive to uncover your strengths and compensate for weaknesses. For example, if you are a cold person, you may be drawn to warm, earthy tones and cuddly warm fabrics, whereas a hot person may be more attracted to cooling greens and icy silky cottons. Don't suppress your natural taste inclinations in order to please others. After all, you are the one who will have to live with the impact of an environment discordant with your senses.

The decor of each vastu shastra-inspired house is as individual as the owners themselves. Despite this, all such houses seem to have a calm ambience,

a simple elegance that comes from uncluttered spaces, and carefully chosen homewares and furniture. Minimalism and space allow energy to circulate freely in the house, whereas clutter and mess create a stagnation of energy. Many people are under the impression that the more we have the happier we are but, as Indian saint Zai Baba has noted, our material desires are just like coins in our pockets, they weigh us down. You could simply walk around your home and ask everything, "Do I really love you?" If the answer is no, out it should go. Then you will be surrounded only by things that you adore.

Colors

The right colors are silent music; the wrong colors irritate and disturb.
Louis Cheskin

Color is a basic human need like fire and water, a raw material indispensable to life.
Fernand Leger, painter

Colors are vibrating waves that have the ability to vitalize, heal and enlighten us. Some blind people can even distinguish a color by feeling its vibration.

The subliminal effects of color on our minds and bodies has been well documented. Patients have been shown to heal more rapidly after operations in a mint-green surgery; a rose-pink room calms psychotic patients; blue suppresses the appetite, whereas red fires it up. The mood of the room and the character of the people spending time there determine which are the best colors to use. In general, muted pastels create a relaxing, sedating mood, and bright colors stimulate and motivate us. Combining colors pleasantly is like good cooking: it is not the individual ingredients that matter, but the synergy they create in combination. You can add a splash of color to the home in many ways — for example, with furnishings, candles, light bulbs and artwork, or by painting the walls, doors and ceilings. A simple rule to keep in mind is to choose light colors if you want to create the feeling of space and light, and darker colors if you want to make a room more defined and subdued.

Certain colors are suitable for specific functions:

Red	Increases energy and appetite. (Use sparingly, as it can promote hyperactivity.)
Orange	Increases intelligence and vitality. Pale apricots and saffrons are favored in vastu shastra.
Yellow	Balances the digestion and elevates moods. (Use in moderation, as yellow is the most fatiguing color for eyes.)
Green	Enhances prana, is calming and promotes harmony. (Can be too cooling.)
Blue	Is sedating, aids communication and promotes contemplation. Suppresses appetite.
Violet	Provides spiritual inspiration and stimulates the mind.
White	Is cleansing, and promotes peace and perception. (Can make you hypersensitive.)
Black	Aids introspection and detachment. (Can attract negativity and feed fears.)
Brown	Brings the grounding, nourishing energies of the earth into the house.

Music

Music gives soul to the universe, wings to the mind, flight to the imagination,
charm to sadness, gaiety and life to everything.
It is the essence of order and leads to all that is good, just and beautiful.
PLATO

Music is medicine for the soul. It nurtures intuition, creativity, imagination, regeneration and joy in our lives. The harmonious vibrations of sound waves can resonate in tune with our biorhythms and create a healing living environment.

Sounds with destructive vibrations can disturb our mental and physical balance, especially when the waves bounce around the closed environment of the home. Television, traffic, machinery and negative music are all sound vibrations that can shatter the peace of a household. One way to counteract this is to fill the home with uplifting sound vibrations, such as the Indian ragas and mantras. Ragas are the musical replication of the expression of the universe. Each raga is a specific melody that evokes a distinct mood unique to a time of day. When you play the raga specific to that time of day, the vibrations in the house will align with the pulse of the surrounding elements.

Sanskrit mantra recordings are also available at music stores. George Harrison describes the mantra as "a mystical energy encased in a sound structure, each mantra containing within its vibrations a unique power." Mantras unleash powerful energies into the atmosphere, creating a serene and vibrant ambience in the home. They also reawaken our dormant spiritual awareness so we can connect with our higher selves and make healthier choices throughout the day. The positive influence of mantras is particularly helpful for people with mental imbalances such as mood swings and addictions. Alternatively, we can reconnect with the earth's vibration by playing recordings of natural phenomena such as ocean waves and rainforest sounds, and of grounding indigenous music.

Raga	Ideal time to play
Raga Lalit, Raga Bhairavi	Morning
Raga Patadeep, Raga Madhuvanti	Noon
Raga Shankara, Raga Durga	Afternoon
Raga Bageswari, Raga Jaijaivanti	Evening

AROMAS

Twenty-four hours a day, we are subliminally affected by the fragrances we inhale. Our sense of smell is a thousand times more sensitive than our sense of taste, and is the only sense that has a direct connection with the brain. An aroma can evoke memories, stimulate primary drives such as hunger and sexuality, and regulate basic bodily functions, including sleep, the stress response and digestion.

Aromatherapy is another way to maximize the nurturing energies of a home. Vastu shastra uses aromatherapy in the home in the form of perfumes, oil lamps, pot pourri, fresh flowers and incense. Only pure essential oils and incense are recommended, as impure forms will simply pollute the atmosphere, contributing to psycho-physiological imbalances. In vastu, it is especially important to have a welcoming scent at the front entrance, a cleansing aroma in the bathroom and a spiritually uplifting fragrance in the north-east corner of the house, or in the meditation area.

The best carrier oil is ghee (clarified butter) or sesame oil.

Home aromas to consider:

Basil, bergamot, chamomile, cinnamon, clary sage, frankincense, Himalayan cedarwood, jasmine, lemon, neroli, rose, sandalwood, vetiver, wintergreen, ylang ylang.

ARTWORK

A piece of art can set the mood for a room, unconsciously altering our state of mind. Happy, unified, spiritually uplifting scenes and sculptures are most strongly recommended in vastu, as the *Mayamata* advises, "representations of joyous scenes and spiritual images." Conversely, artwork that depicts scenes of war, fights, death, demons, black magic, giants, weeping, distressed people, poverty, terror, disasters, or vicious animals is said to bring misfortune.

Auspicious Elements

Any object subject to veneration receives "vibrations"
or psychic energetic impulses, and, once charged, retains them.
MARK BALFOUR, THE SIGN OF THE SERPENT

We invest objects with meaning according to our past conditioning and present mental associations. The decor that is auspicious for your particular home will be dependent on your individual, spiritual and aesthetic tastes. If you don't find Chinese-style feng shui-inspired items attractive, you may prefer the Indian- and Tibetan-inspired items of vastu shastra. Remember not to place these items on the floor, in the bathroom with a toilet or in an area where your feet will point directly at them, as this is considered disrespectful.

Prayer flags	Often inscribed with prayers that are symbolically carried up to the heavens by the wind.
Conch	A symbol of victory and timelessness. The element ether is purified by its primordial vibration, likened to the mantra "aum."
Lotus	Our true nature and our qualities are said to blossom when we reach for higher wisdom, just as the lotus blossoms when it reaches for the sky.
Lamps	Brass ghee lamps are ideal, but small candles can be substituted. The flame is symbolic of inner wisdom and enlightenment.
Four masks	Traditionally used in the Indian state of Tamil Nadu, each mask is placed on the outside of the house; each faces a main direction (north, south, east, or west). The masks act as guardians for each region.

Representations of Shri Krishna	The flute-playing god who cultivates love and devotion in the heart.
Representations of Shri Rama	The incarnation of righteousness (dharma). The archetypal ruler. Good for managers, leaders and politicians.
Representations of Shri Narashimha	Half man/half lion god who protects the virtuous from danger.
Representations of Shri Ganesha	Pot-bellied elephant god who removes obstacles to progress.
Representations of Shri Hanuman	Monkey god who helps humans to develop strength and persistence.
Representations of Shri Laksmi	The goddess of wealth, who guards the females of the house and brings prosperity.
Representations of Shri Vishnu	God who sustains the universe, merciful to those who make offerings to him.
Representations of Shri Shiva	The third of the trinity. Hailed as the ideal Yogi; single women often pray to him for a good husband, and he also grants the discipline and dedication required for performing spiritual penance.
Representations of Shri Saraswati	The goddess of learning and the arts.
Representations of Lord Buddha	His presence will bring serenity, peace and contemplation into a home.
Yantras	Powerful symbols that embody the geometric harmony of the universe.
Tulasi, lotus, or rudraksha beads	Holy beads associated respectively with Shri Krishna, Lord Buddha and Shri Shiva.

The Garden

Very much like painting or sculpture, gardening is a means of giving physical, sensory form to emotional or spiritual matters.
MARC P. KEANE

Green gardens offer a healing haven from the artificial surroundings of modern living. To many they are a sanctuary where, through the revitalizing connection with nature, sanity and serenity are restored. There is a saying that people who plant bountiful gardens will enjoy the positive fruits of their actions.

A beautiful garden certainly lifts the mood and image of a house immeasurably, creating a paradise on earth. It also frames views, offers shelter from the elements, absorbs noise and invites visits from the animal kingdom. Plants create fresh air by absorbing carbon monoxide and some chemical fumes, as well as by countering positive ions created by electrical appliances and powerlines. They release rejuvenating oxygen, moisture and uplifting fragrances, which permeate the house. They attract and trap particles such as lead, mold, dust and soot outside and inside of the house. Flowering and sacred plants are also advisable, as the flowers can be used for decorating the house and for daily rituals. Culinary plants give a degree of nutritional self-sufficiency and a flavor burst that cannot be bought.

A Gorgeous Garden

It is important to keep the garden path clear and the garden free of old pots, rotting woods and weeds. Clearing out the old to make way for fresh life is a metaphor for residents' receptiveness to growth and abundance.

The garden path should wind gently rather than going straight to the front door. Any sculptures or pictures in the garden should not depict fierce animals or sad scenes. Gentle, friendly, contemplative forms are best.

Landscaping plans in vastu shastra are dictated by the Purusha mandala and solar science. Larger trees should not be planted too close to the house, as their roots are an obvious danger to the house's foundations. They are preferable in the south or west of the house, offering protection from the damaging afternoon rays. Culinary herbs and plants are preferable in the north-west, and medicinal or sacred plants in the north-east. Never plant a tree in the middle of the house — this will prevent spiritual blessings from entering your life.

The few plants that are not recommended in vastu shastra are thorny trees, those with milk sap, plants with stunted growth, such as bonsai or trees in pots, stolen plants, vegetation from cemeteries, and spiky trees that look like spears.

Many plants are considered auspicious, but bear in mind that not all of them are suitable for every climate and condition. Beneficial plants mentioned in vastu texts include the following:

Banana: A rejuvenative and stomachic fruit whose leaves can also be used as plates.

Coconut: (*Cocus nucifera*) The coconut, with its three layers of shell, flesh and water, represents the sheaths of the cosmos and the subtle body. It is best in the south-west region of the property.

Fig tree: Renowned for its stabilizing and protective influence, this is the tree under which Buddha reached enlightenment. Plant *Ficus arnottiana* in the north of the property, *Ficus bengalensis* in the east, *Ficus racemosus* in the south and *Ficus religiosa* in the west.

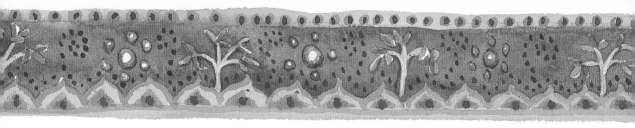

Holy basil: (*Ocimum sanctum*) Hailed as a panacea, tulasi, as it is known in India, is a sacred tree with amazing healing properties. It is used in over 300 Ayurvedic medicines for scores of conditions. Inhaling air which has passed through this plant is said to purify the nadis (subtle channels) of the body. It is used in the worshipping of Shri Krishna.

Jackfruit: (*Artocarpus heterophyllus*) A male tonic fruit which has anti-viral properties, being trialed for the treatment of AIDS.

Mango: (*Mangiflora indica*) Called the king of fruits. The leaves and fruit are used in sacred ceremonies.

Neem: (*Azadirachta indica*) Ideally planted in the west, neem has anti-parasitic, anti-bacterial and anti-fungal properties. Chewing a few neem leaves a day is said to keep the blood pure and digestion strong. The frayed twigs can be used for a toothbrush.

Other useful herbs and flowering plants:
Amrita: (*Tinospora cordifolia*) Meaning "immortality," this very hardy plant is excellent for improving circulation and alleviating arthritis.

Ashoka: (*Saraca ashoka*) A sturdy cooling tree, good for conditions such as bleeding and disorders of the female reproductive system.

Betel: (*Piper betle*) Useful as a bronchodilator and digestive. Can be chewed after eating to improve digestion and absorption.

Bilva: (*Aegle marmelos*) A spiritual tree whose leaves are used to make garlands

for Lord Shiva. Highly medicinal, especially for stabilizing the stomach and for metabolic functions.

Coriander: (*Coriandrum sativum*) A cooling herb, good for the eyes and bladder.

Curry: (*Murraya koenigii*) A large, hardy tree; the leaves are excellent for the digestion.

Eucalyptus: (genus *Eucalyptus*) Ideally planted in the west of the home. The oil is anti-bacterial, acting as a powerful air purifier.

Frangipani: (genus *Plumeria*) A very sturdy tree whose flowers intoxicate with their sweet fragrance. Ideal for making garlands.

Gardenia: (*Gardenia gumnifera*) A beautiful, fragrant flower.

Ginger: (*Zingiber officinalis*) Used widely in Indian and Chinese herbal medicine to improve the circulation, reduce pain and allay nausea.

Gooseberry: (*Phyllanthus emblica*) The most powerful rejuvenative and anti-oxidant used in Ayurveda.

Jasmine: (*Jasminum sambac*) This plant's sweet fragrance is said to calm the mind.

Rose: (*Rosa canina*) Rose flowers are perfect for flower arrangements and as a morning offering.

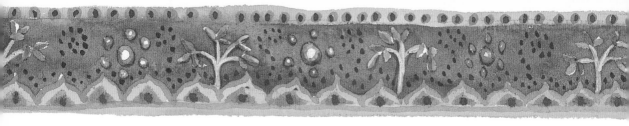

Saffron: (*Crocus sativus*) This improves immunity and vitality.

Sandalwood: (*Santanum album*) This takes some time to mature, but, once it does, can be used to create your own pure incense.

Shatavari: (*Asparagus racemosus*) This literally means "a hundred husbands," a name indicative of the plant's female reproductive properties. A rejuvenative plant ideal for decorating garden fences.

Shirisham: (*Albizzia lebbek*) A strong anti-poison herb, used for all kinds of internal and external poisons of organic and animal origin.

Turmeric: (*Curcuma longa*) Indispensable in cooking, turmeric is a wonderful liver tonic and blood cleanser.

Water lotus: (*Nelumbo nucifera*) A beautiful garden feature which gives off a heavenly fragrance. Spiritually, it symbolizes the human capacity to rise above material entanglement to reach enlightenment.

WONDERFUL WATER FEATURES

The soothing sound of waves gently lapping against the shore, a gently bubbling brook, or a trickling fountain can wash away all our tensions and cleanse our mind of worries. Water is a refreshing, revitalizing and cooling addition to a garden. Today, with the ready availability of small submersible water pumps, anyone can have a small water feature in the garden. The ideal place for a pond or pool is in the north-east of the garden or room, preferably on the north wall. The water can flow directly toward the house, or from east to west or west to east. This will generate negative ions to keep the air fresh. Some vastu masters

advise that a water feature above ground is more suited in the south-west. Water on the roof is said to drown all future aspirations.

If you don't have a small fountain, try putting a turtle or frogs in your pond to reduce stagnation. Be careful not to allow aquatic vegetation to totally cover the water, as this can prove a practical danger to infants. Ideally, the water feature should not touch the compound wall, and it should not directly face the front door.

In vastu shastra the shape of the pool or pond is generally square or rectangular; this is evident in all ancient temple bathing pools. However, since wells are generally round, it is acceptable to have a small round or kidney-shaped water feature.

The reflective quality of water can provide a lovely mirror for the house and garden, as exemplified by the Taj Mahal pool. However, the pool should not be so large as to overshadow the house as this will override the stabilizing earth element and cause instability in the home.

Vastu Shastra for Clinics and Learning Centers

THE CLINIC

It is becoming more common for therapists to run clinics from home. Basic vastu guidelines can be implemented in order to do this in a way that is practical, professional and comfortable.

A clear, tidy and well-lit entrance with two plants on either side of the front door will offer a bright welcome. Entrances for residents and clients should ideally be separate. The waiting area can have fresh drinking water and reading materials, and be situated near a bathroom with a toilet. Gentle music should play in the south-east of the consulting room. The actual consulting room is best located in the west or north-west of the house. The treatment room should always be well-ventilated and decorated with fresh flowers. Keep a subtle scent burning.

The therapist should face west, with the patient facing east. Arrange the bed so that patients lying down will have their heads toward the east, south, or west. The therapist's framed credentials should be on the east wall. Money is ideally kept in the north or east wall so the safe opens to the north.

THE LEARNING CENTER

Using vastu shastra principles to organize educational centers will enhance the concentration of students and the efficiency of the staff.

Room placement should be as follows:

- The classroom should ideally be in the north-east region.
- The board in the classroom should face west so that students face east.
- The school library is best located in the west.
- A principal's room in the south-west will command respect.
- The staff room should be in the north-west.
- The accounts department can be placed in the north or east.
- The playground is best located in the east or north.
- A canteen in the south-east is good vastu shastra.
- If there are dormitory rooms, these should be in the south or south-west, with heads of beds facing east or south.
- The assembly, meeting, or conference hall would be perfect in the north.

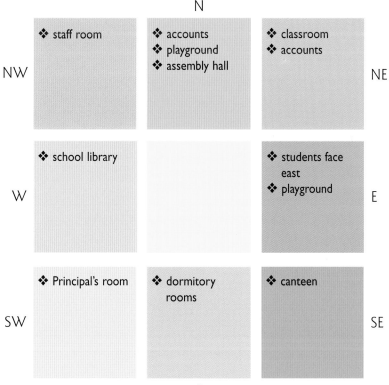

Healing the Home

Where the violence done to nature is great, or the elements introduced
so out of accord with the landscape, the wound will never heal.
STEPHAN SKINNER IN THE LIVING EARTH MANUAL OF FENG SHUI

SICK BUILDINGS

Modern advances have given us a much larger scope for ease and enjoyment in life, but they have also introduced a wave of harmful toxins into the home. Are we living in death-traps or coffins rather than in nurturing homes? The United States Environmental Protection Agency has discovered over 1000 pollutants in the home, 60 of which are linked to cancer. Many other toxins have been linked to increases in asthma, eczema, chronic fatigue, insomnia and hyperactivity.

The accumulation of chemical vapors, synthetic building materials and electromagnetic fields, combined with poor ventilation and artificial lighting, have created a modern phenomenon known as the "sick building syndrome." This occurs when the building that is meant to protect us is actually destroying us. To prevent this, try to avoid dangers from gases and vapors, particles, and radiation and electromagnetic fields.

Coping with toxic gases and vapors

As far as possible, avoid using kerosene or paraffin and bottled gas heaters. Rather, use flued gas burners, which can be vented to the outside and have sealed combustion chambers. Alternatively, use electric heaters. Allow good ventilation around heaters and stoves. Have as many indoor and outdoor plants as possible to absorb the fumes. Contact the local health and safety authorities or an air quality consultant to assess levels of radon, carbon monoxide, or ozone in the region. Avoid the use of toxic varnishes, resins, binders, fungicides, insecticides, paints, stainers, adhesives and plastics in construction.

Here is a list of the worst culprits, their side-effects, and ways to counteract them.

Gases and vapors	Side effects
Radon: natural inert gas present in certain geological regions, carried into the house by dust, natural gas or water.	Damage to lung tissue, linked to cancer.
Carbon monoxide, nitric oxide and carbon dioxide: formed from incomplete combustion of gas flames from cookers or unflued heaters. Carbon monoxide is from vehicle exhausts.	Respiratory, nervous and circulatory system disorders. First signs of toxicity may include nausea, headaches, dizziness and breathlessness.
Organochlorines: these include polychlorinated biphenyls, polyvinyl chloride (plastic), turpentine, ammonia, acetone, naphthalene (in mothballs), chlorine (in bleach), phenols (in plastics, cleaning agents, synthetic resins), chloroform and chloramines (present in household cleaning products). Lindane, pentachlorophenol and tributyl tin oxide are toxic pesticides and fungicides used to preserve timbers.	Potentially carcinogenic, irritates all mucous membranes, headaches, nausea, mood changes. Linked to skin, respiratory and nervous system disorders.
Formaldehyde: used to bond timber and plastics, also as preservative for paper and textiles. Also present in combustion of heating appliances, and tobacco.	Irritates mucous membranes, leading to allergies, headaches, hayfever, nosebleeds. A suspected carcinogen.

Coping with toxic particles

These toxins will generally be a problem when you move into an established home. Asbestos, lead pipes, cadmium paint and any other dangerous materials must be removed by special contractors. Trying to move them yourself will pose serious health hazards.

Particles	Side effects
Asbestos: fibrous material formerly used for insulation and fire-proofing.	Asbestosis and cancer.
Metals: aluminum (from cookware), copper (from water pipes), lead (in old water pipes), cadmium (from paints).	Toxic levels of these metals are linked to chronic fatigue syndrome, neuromuscular disorders, Alzheimer's disease and a vast variety of other illnesses.
Fungi, bacteria, molds, dust, dust mites and miscellaneous microorganisms. Air conditioning and poor cleanliness. Synthetic fabrics, feathers, hair and down bedding, ("hair bedding" OK) carpets, animals and upholstery.	Allergies and infections, asthma, irritability.

Air conditioning should be checked, cleaned and maintained. Try to implement natural ventilation alternatives. Replace carpets with wood, tiles, marble or slate. Curtains can be replaced with blinds or louvers. Fit bedding with dust-mite protective covers. Treat any existing fabric or carpets by steam cleaning, and use a natural dust-mite terminator. Wood-slat mattress bases are preferable to spring-base beds. Try to fit closets (cupboards) that reach from floor to ceiling, with no gaps for microorganisms to breed in. Wallpaper traps dust and encourages mold; paint is better. To eliminate dust mites, wash all bed linen in temperatures over 55°F. The first line of defense against air-borne allergens is keeping your house clean and well ventilated.

Coping with radiation and electromagnetic fields

Have levels and sources of radon and radium assessed. If levels are high, seal the sources of contamination, increase natural ventilation and install radon detectors. Monitor levels regularly. Check microwaves for leaks; and consider other cooking methods. Avoid fluorescent and halogen lights. To reduce exposure to ultraviolet light, use glass, and protect the house from sun by high trees in the south-west.

Radiation and electromagnetic fields	Side effects
Radiation exposure: generally from a natural source such as radon or radium bearing building materials — for example, earth, stone, pumice, granite, concrete, bricks, alum shale, calcium silicate slag and uranium. Proximity to a nuclear power station will often cause higher levels of radiation.	Increased risk of cancer.
Microwave ovens: radiation can leak from poorly sealed microwaves.	Possible link with leukemia being investigated.
Ultra-violet rays: fluorescent light fittings may contain toxic PCBs (polychlorinated biphenyls). Fluorescent lights also radiate higher electromagnetic fields than other light sources. Glass shields us from levels of UV-A and UV-B, but windows, doors and skylights made from plastics such as polycarbonate and acrylics do not filter out UV radiations.	Skin cancer, headaches, eyestrain, irritability, fatigue, weakness and tinnitis.
Electromagnetic fields: emanate from the earth & from electrically charged technology. The earth's natural electromagnetic field, pulsing at 7.83 beats per seconds, is a healthy influence on humans. Astronauts in space, deprived of the earth's electromagnetic field, have become mentally confused and physically disoriented. These fields are beneficial, but some scientists warn that staying for many hours over a conjunction of lay lines can lead to geopathic stress, a syndrome linked to an increased rate in many diseases, including cancer. Unnatural electromagnetic fields created by electrical appliances, such as visual display units, alarms clocks, sound systems and lights, and all wiring, generally pulse from 50–60 cycles per second, and are detrimental in ways becoming apparent only now.	Symptoms of electrostress may include increased risk of cancer and leukemia, high blood pressure, insomnia, nausea, headaches, and irritability and other psychological disturbances.

LIVING WELL

Like the lotus that thrives in the mud, the potential for realisation
grows in the rich soil of our everyday lives.
HH DALAI LAMA

The way we live in our homes is just as important as the homes themselves. Vastu shastra shares many of the precepts of Ayurveda and Yoga in guiding us toward a more fulfilling lifestyle.

Ten daily observances are advised for creating good karma and leading a positive life.

The ten daily observances	Name
Non-violence through compassion	ahimsa
Honesty and truthfulness	satya
Non-stealing	astheya
Control of the senses	brahmacarya
Selflessness	aparigraha
Cleanliness	sauca
Contentment with what you have been given	santosha
Austerity	tapas
Study of spiritual truths	swadhyaya
Surrender to the will of the divine	ishwara pranidhana

DAILY RITUALS FOR CLEANING AND HEALING

Nature never denies its bounties to those who want to be near it and worship it.
PROF V.V. RAMAN, VASTU SHASTRA SCHOLAR

Our role as guardians of the earth is a privilege that we should honor by an attitude of gratitude and responsibility. According to vastu shastra, every particle of creation is sacred, and brimming with life force. One way to recognize the divinity inherent in every atom is by practicing simple rituals. These rituals give us a deeper bond with our homes and cleanse them of any bad influences. When we learn to see the sacred essence of our actions, every day becomes a "holy day." Even simple daily routines can be invested with meaning when we view them from a spiritual perspective.

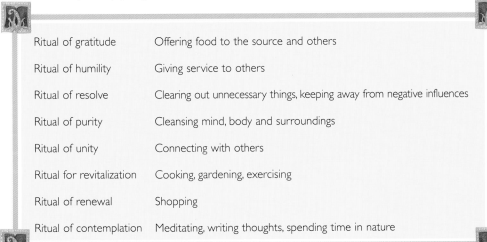

Ritual of gratitude	Offering food to the source and others
Ritual of humility	Giving service to others
Ritual of resolve	Clearing out unnecessary things, keeping away from negative influences
Ritual of purity	Cleansing mind, body and surroundings
Ritual of unity	Connecting with others
Ritual for revitalization	Cooking, gardening, exercising
Ritual of renewal	Shopping
Ritual of contemplation	Meditating, writing thoughts, spending time in nature

CLEARING THE HOUSE'S ENERGY

Have you ever entered a house where you felt you could cut the air with a knife? What you were probably feeling was an accumulation of "psychic dross." Just as our minds and bodies collect mental and physical toxins over time, so does a house accumulate a distinct energy. The character and physical state of the people in a house can leave a vibrational impression on the house that can disturb us if we don't clear it. These vibrations can have quite a significant impact on us, particularly if we are in a house that has had negative occupants previously. We can start to take on negative attitudes or even the physical illnesses of past residents without realizing the connection.

Therefore it is a good idea, before moving into a new place, to clear the house's energy yourself or to employ a professional Hindu priest or space clearer.

Procedure for house clearing yourself

First you will need to remove any physical toxicity by clearing the house and garden of any clutter.

Then, using water and sandalwood, or lemon essential oil, wipe down all places that previous tenants would have touched, such as door knobs, stove knobs, taps and the letterbox. Clean the floors, walls and closets (cupboards). If you are living in a new home you can still do this even though no one else has ever lived here before. This will help to clear energy from past negative issues such as arguments, illnesses, depression, thefts and even deaths.

Physical clutter causes mental clutter and also blocks the house's circulation, preventing fresh vitality from flowing through. Take time to clear things from each room, not forgetting to look under beds and in drawers. Many people find that once they start they feel so light and liberated they don't want to stop. As Thoreau said, "Our life is frittered away by detail ... simplify ... simplify ...."

Brush away cobwebs and dust, and attend to basic things such as missing light bulbs. Once this is complete, set up an altar as described in "The Inner Sanctum" on page 39.

Once this is complete, the ritual itself is ideally carried out at sunrise, or in the morning before 10. Make holy water as described on page 76. After bathing and dressing in fresh clothes, take a bell in your left hand and holy water in your right. Opening all of your windows and doors, walk to the east side of the home and face east. It is preferable to do this outside, but if you are in an apartment building the ritual can be carried out inside. Ring the bell gently while reciting three times the following mantra to Indra, the guardian of the east:

"Prachyai Dishi Indraya Namaha."

Then spray a little holy water on the ground. Resume ringing the bell while you walk to the south side of the house, then face the south and chant thrice:

"Dakshinau Dishi Yamaya Namaha"

Spray holy water in this direction. Ringing the bell, walk to the west side of the house and face west, reciting three times:

"Paschime Dishi Varunaya Namaha"

Still ringing the bell, walk to the north side of the house and chant three times:

"Uttarau dishi Khuberaya Namaha"

Then go to the north-east corner where the shrine is set up, and carry out the elemental recharge as explained in the following section. After everything is complete, make a nice meal, offer it to the Vastu Purusha, and then serve it to the other residents of the house.

RECHARGING THE ELEMENTS

Even though you may lead a very busy life, it is worth taking five minutes every morning to energize the elemental balance in your home. This very simple yet profound practice channels supportive energies into your life so your day will be much smoother and easier to cope with. Many households in India, Bali and Asia practice this ritual every morning.

The best time to recharge the elements is before breakfast, after you have gone to the toilet, brushed your teeth, had a shower and dressed in fresh clothes.

Set aside a small area of your home, as described in "The Inner Sanctum" page 39. All of the utensils you use should preferably not be used for any other purpose.

You will need the following articles:

- A bell, preferably with a deep ring or a conch shell (optional)
- Lighter or matches
- Three sticks of pure incense
- An incense holder
- A small candle or lamp, to which you may add ½ tsp camphor crystals
- A small open container of water
- A fresh, sweet-smelling, stemless flower

Do not smell or taste any of the articles before the ceremony. To endow the water with increased spiritual potency, chant the following mantra over it three times:

"Gange ca Yamune caive Godavari Sarasvati
Narmade Sindho Kaveri jale 'smin sannidhim kuru"
(May water from the holy rivers Ganges, Yamuna, Godavari, Saraswati, Narmada,
Sindhu and Kaveri kindly be present in this water.)

Then chant "aum" over the water eight times. The water will now be considered holy, and as such will have powerful purifying properties.

Ideally, your symbol of divinity should be placed in such a way that you are near an open window in the north-east or east. This symbol acts as a medium, accepting your offerings and passing them on to the spirit of the home, Vastu Purusha.

1 Placing your palms together in prayer position, sense the vibration in your body.
2 Visualize a protective white aura enveloping the house, including yourself. You may also pray for your divinity's presence to pervade the home.
3 Ring the bell in your left hand in three clockwise circles around the divinity, or blow the conch shell three times. This will purify the element of ether.
4 Light the three sticks of incense, holding them in your right hand. Ring the bell in your left hand while offering the incense clockwise around the divinity for three circles. Then place the incense in the holder. This will purify the element of air.
5 Light the candle or lamp and, ringing the bell in your left hand, offer the flame in three clockwise circles. This will purify the fire element.
6 Ringing the bell in your left hand, hold the water in your right hand and offer it three times around the divinity. You can then place the water at the base of the picture or statue and sprinkle a little water on the flower with the fingers of your right hand.
7 Offering the flower in three clockwise circles, ring the bell with your left hand.
8 Place the flower in front of the divinity.

You can now recite an appropriate prayer of your choice. Here are two simple ones to guide you:

*Please protect and nurture this household so that we may always be
healthy, wealthy and wise.*

May this home overflow with light, love and laughter always.

The elements will now be revitalized, and you can enjoy them directly by smelling the incense and flower, drinking some water or placing a drop on the crown of your head. Sit now and gaze at the flame.

Conclusion

With the earth's environmental crises and the rapid rise in criminal behavior, everything may seem overwhelmingly hopeless. Anything we do in this life is like a pebble thrown into a still pond — creating ripples that effect a change in the whole environment. Those who realize this are taking on board the philosophy of acting locally while thinking globally.

We should start by honoring ourselves, our immediate home environment and those close to us. Respect for ourselves is reflected in the respect we have for our living environment and for those with whom we share it. By cherishing and nurturing these gifts, we will have a stable core for effecting lasting changes. Children growing up in happy and conscious homes will be more integrated adults who value the necessity of healthier air, water, fire and earth. Vastu shastra's message is that we need to prioritize these issues if we are to survive as a species. Its wisdom aims to make us aware of our total dependence on the environment so that we can learn to live in harmony with it, creating an oasis from chaos. May we all live in accordance with natural laws so that health and happiness flourishes in every household.

Glossary

Note: All gods mentioned in this list are Hindu gods.

Agni god governing the fire element
Ayurveda Indian medical science
Brahma god who is considered the father of all creatures and the creator of the material universe
Chi life force energy permeating everything
Cosmological theory the theory that the universe is uniform and homogenous and that the planets and forces in the universe have a divine order that impacts upon the Earth
Dharma righteous living
Durga goddess who destroys evil and protects piety
Electromagnetic energy electric waves emanating naturally from the earth or artificially from appliances
Epsom salts bath salts, generally consisting of sodium bicarbonate and sodium carbonate
Feng shui Chinese system of design and placement; literally means wind and water
Ganesha elephant-headed god who removes obstacles placed in the path of good ventures and obstructs the path of negative influences
Geomancer a specialist on the energy fields impacted on the Earth
Geopathic stress a state resulting from exposure to distorted electromagnetic fields emanating from the earth
Ida feminine, "yin" energy channel in the body
Indra god who controls the weather, particularly thunder and rain
Jyotish Indian term for "astrologer," literally "one who lights the way"
Karma the law of cause and effect, action and result
Kirlian photography a method of photographing subtle energy fields
Krishna god who personifies pure, unconditional loving relationships; known for his compassion and playfulness
Kubera the god of wealth
Kum kum vermilion powder (a dye)
Laksmi the goddess of fortune
Mahabharata an ancient Indian epic
Mandala geometric diagram that acts as a sacred guide
Maya a celestial architect; can also mean "illusion"
Navagraha Homam a special worship to balance the imbalances caused by malevolent planets

Pandavas the five brothers who feature prominently in the epic Mahabharata, which includes the Bhagavad-Gita

Pingala the masculine right-sided energy channel in the body

Praayama yogic breathing exercises

Prana life-force energy permeating everything

Raga classical Indian musical melody

Rama god who personifies nobility and ideal leadership

Ramayana the ancient epic story of Rama

Rangoli also known as "kolam;" the sacred design drawn on the ground at a home, usually at a threshold

Saraswati goddess of learning and the arts

Shastra science or body of knowledge

Sick building syndrome an illness resulting from exposure to a toxic, unhealthy building

Solar science the study of the effect of the sun in the solar system and on the earth

Sthapatya-Veda the original text containing details of vastu shastra

Symbiosis a close connection and relationship between interdependent things

Sthapati a master knowledgeable in all aspects of the science of vastu

Terrestrial relating to the land, earth

Varuna god of water controlling the oceans, waves and rivers

Vastu dwelling or primal form of something

Vastu pooja worship of the home

Vastu Purusha the spirit that embodies a site

Vayu god of the element wind; also known as Maruti

Veedhi shoolas literally "road arrows" or roads that terminate at the home

Vishnu father of Brahma and preserver of the universe

Vishvakarma the divine architect who built many famous ancient structures

Yama the god of death and justice; also known as Dharmaraja — king of dharma

Yantra mystical diagram that represents and attracts divine energy

Published by Lansdowne Publishing Pty Ltd
Level 1, 18 Argyle Street, Sydney NSW 2000, Australia

First published 2000

© Copyright text, illustrations and design:
Lansdowne Publishing 2000

Commissioned by: Deborah Nixon
Production Manager: Sally Stokes
Project Co-ordinator: Alexandra Nahlous
Editor: Avril Janks
Designer: Sue Rawkins
Illustrator: Penny Lovelock

Set in Stempel Schneidler on QuarkXPress

Printed in Singapore by Tien Wah Press (Pte) Ltd

National Library of Cataloguing-in-Publication data

Robertson, Caroline
Vastu shastra.

ISBN 1 86302 697 5.
1. House construction - India. 2. Architecture, Domestic - India.
3. Astrology and architecture - India. 4. Architecture, Hindu - India. I. Title.

720.954